The Hook

For Annette, Joe and Lucas

Also by Duncan Bush

Poetry
Masks

Novels
The Genre of Silence
Glass Shot

The Hook

Duncan Bush

seren

seren
is the book imprint of
Poetry Wales Press Ltd
Wyndham Street, Bridgend, Wales

© Duncan Bush, 1997

ISBN 1-85411-203-1

A CIP record for this title is available from
the British Library

All rights reserved. No part of this publication may be reproduced,
stored in a retrieval system, or transmitted at any time or by any means
electronic, mechanical, photocopying, recording or otherwise
without the prior permission of the copyright holder.

*The publisher works with the financial assistance of the
Arts Council of Wales*

Printed in Palatino by The Cromwell Press, Melksham

Contents

vii   *Introduction*

from *Aquarium*

- 11   Ulysses Becalmed
- 14   Soleil de Miel
- 16   Girl on the Beach, Cannes
- 17   Falsetto
- 19   Chanson de l'Après-Midi
- 20   Criseyde's Dream
- 21   Angoisse
- 22   Sisera and Jael
- 23   Gwlad, Gwlad
- 24   Gothic Cathedral
- 26   Aquarium du Trocadéro
- 28   Snake Park, Kenya
- 30   Fatherhood
- 31   Vanishing Point 3000
- 33   Nausea
- 34   Snow at Dawn
- 35   Near Tilbury Dock
- 37   Old Man in Scrumpy House
- 39   Saloon Bar Drinker
- 40   Agony
- 41   The Avatar of King David
- 42   Widow
- 43   Mississippi
- 46   The Sunflower
- 47   A Sense of the Passing
- 48   Revolt
- 49   A Generation
- 50   Tristia: a Poem for St David's Day
- 52   Movietone
- 54   Poem for Joseph, 10 days old
- 55   Poem for Joe, December

from *Black Faces, Red Mouths*

59 Pneumoconiosis
60 Summer, 1984
62 Onllwyn, West Glamorgan, 1985
64 Miner, Abercynon, 1985
65 In the Aftermath

from *Salt*

69 The Hook
71 October Oaks
72 Drainlayer
73 Ramsey Island
76 Pig-Farmer
79 Hill Farmer, Staring into his Fire
81 New Land
82 Quarries at Dinorwic
85 Navvies
96 Cold-Chisel
97 *From* Lament of the Mechanical Excavator
100 Oxford Poems
103 Tartan Army
105 August. Sunday. Gravesend.
108 Back to Cardiff
110 Living
111 Evening
112 Hot Estate Sunday
113 Cafe, Rainy Tuesday Morning
115 Pull-in

117 *Notes*
119 *Acknowledgements*

Introduction

This volume is, predominantly, a reissue of two collections of poetry, *Aquarium* and *Salt*, which were first published over a decade ago (in 1983 and 1985 respectively) and have since fallen out of print. I've taken the opportunity to revise a number of the poems. As Paul Valéry put it, "A poem is never finished. It is only abandoned". In this spirit, I've made a number of corrections of detail and recast one or two poems more substantially. Revision is, however, a delicate process, and best adopted with caution. As a poet gets older and publishes more widely, the critical faculty becomes more developed. Normally this is to the good. In poetry, as in other walks of life, it's common to feel occasional embarrassment at an earlier simplemindedness. But pruning away at the apparent excesses in work written when one's talent was, if not richer in inspiration, then more youthful and enthusiastic, can remove something integral. I can think of several instances of poets who in trying to make some of their best earlier poems fitting to a more senior status have ended up by emasculating them.

Of course, to the cold eye of hindsight, several poems in the books on which this collection is based, have seemed beyond saving. What appears to happen with bad poems — as with clothes, furniture, badly designed cars — is not just that their technical faults become apparent but that, a decade later, they suddenly look hopelessly dated. In these instances I've been tempted to rewrite so radically that I've been confronted with the choice of either publishing a new poem or excluding the old one. In two cases I've found myself writing a new and quite different poem in response, as it were, to my sense of the inadequacies of the old one. One poem I've dropped altogether.

Duncan Bush, 1997

From *Aquarium*

Ulysses Becalmed

"They were born to the soft life
with the wet-nurse's milk,
the finical, dynastic forenames,
all these rich young men:
for them now there is no other — spending
summers at the coast and New Year
on the ski-slopes, a certain cruel,
childish glamour
comes a right, doubt an impossibility....
Look how they sprawl there, grouped
by noon, by shade splashed
water-dark
on the blankness of the beach,
with girls, aperitifs...."

The thatched sunshade's the grizzled silver
of his four-day drunkard's beard,
while their lives seem as crowded
and adventurous as lives glimpsed
in a myth or an advertisement —
each of them born with silver keys in hand
to flats in town and villas on the littoral,
to speedboats and handmade Italian cars:
so many keys to open women.

There is no coming of age
to their extended, playboy adolescence:
only age....

"I too had fewer worries
than the gods until I went to god-built Troy.
Life was a credit-card cashed in on youth
against my father's name. I left a young
wife constant as the speed of light,
a boy of two,
to fight for someone else's slut.

Now dicing for my bed
in Ithaca are beaux like these. I sit
becalmed and numb in gin, watching
their moneyed, actor's ease, and envy
them, wanting their girls.

                                        Once,
in other lives, I had them, had
them all — young whores
too classy, too expensive to be bought, they
wanted me for who I was: a man
invited everywhere, who travelled
in straight lines.... They loved me with
awe-struck ruthlessness,
were pure romantics, arrivistes
still breathless with the jostle for arrival.

That was long ago.... I was a king's son,
and I lived my life in profile
like a matador.
Now nostalgia drags me down. I've lost
direction and my days fly faster
than a weaver's shuttle."

                                    His glass
dabs small, closed circles,
Olympic rings in spillage
on the counter-top.

"Heraclitus knew it, saw
the hunter turning into quarry
in the turning
of the vase. Ten years
I fought in Troy. Ten years
I've swum against this sea —
to stalk the bars along this dock.

Now I'm a myth
crazed on a wine-cup.
There's no going home."

                              Idle,
he sits and weighs the chainweight
of his tether's slack,
his belly's hang. He's far
away and passing middle age,
and Ithaca is further than the womb.

Soleil de Miel

Sunstrain. Gravel; scraggy
dunes. The matchflame flares

invisibly,
to a warped, smoky

transparency. I light
another dry, unwanted mid-afternoon

cigarette: a blind man's
under this blue

sky. I lounge at length
beside you,

dulled
with wine, amnesic

from the sun.
The sea

shudders,
is as far as a mirage. The crowds

are far,
as numerous as sand.

The simple life.... But even

here
we are here

to consume: sun, watermelon,
wine; this tobacco harsh and black as tea;

each other.
The cigarette end smoulders

in sunlight. I shift
to speak to you but you seem

asleep, spent
to the sun. I watch you

through Polaroids.

The scrotum
shrinks.

Hester, we're clenching fistfuls
of loose sand;

they pour out the faster
the tighter we grip.

Girl on the Beach, Cannes

Counting time and his approach in grains of sand;
the beach, the afternoon, are dry sand running
through an hourglass:

your posed recumbency, scantclad, leanmuscled; open
like a bar. A profile of a bored child watches
the tideless sea.

The shouts of shoreline bathers are unreal; they echo
like cries under the glassed roof
of the Piscine.

The waterproofed gold Omega ticks round
on his hairy, tendinous wrist. Briefly
his eyes countenance

the families in striped suntraps; younger men;
his teakbrown, slackening bulk. A hawker
sells. A child scythes sand.

He brushes lightly sanded legs, sits up; slowly
puts on a shirt. He feels blood flutter
to your skin, along your

thin, brown, nerveless body; feels the blood thud
in his chest. Decisive, famous, musclebound,
he clambers to his feet.

You will pass through his strong, dry hands
lithe as an eel and leaping like a salmon;
uttering cries.

Falsetto

Esterina,
twenty autumns rear

like cumulus in the slow, blue
skies above the sea,

departed springtimes
wind you

round their little finger
like a thread. You seek

an end of it, and you
are not afraid.

The maze of dubious tomorrows
doesn't trouble you.

Graceful,
in the trembling heat,

you stretch out on a rock
shining with salt.

You are
like the basking lizard and,

for you, youth lies in wait; for him,
a boy's grass noose.

The sea
tests and renews you; it purifies

and heals
you, like a cut,

and we see you emerge
from it

as chaste and predatory as a Diana. But
your gaiety

already involves
the future, like last night.

A shrug of your
shoulders sheds it like a towel. Suddenly,

laughing, you
run along the springboard, above

the shouting whirlpool. You
hesitate

there, poise
in profile, then you fling

yourself
jackknifed into the arms of that divinity

your lover,
and he takes you....

The springboard
quivers

like a bowstring, and the thread
is burnt.

A glitter
watches from our shaded tables.

(After Montale)

Chanson de l'Après-Midi

Jeanne, your beige skin gives off perfume
heavy as a censer's, to excite
and agitate me, like the night
the voyeur chafing in his room....

I'm lost. All day you sidle
through my thought, fevered with waiting —
and I spend my night prostrating
like a bent priest at an idol.

One sidelong, sly glance from your eyes
incites me, like some roué's potion....
I drown in you like the ocean,
whose caress could make the dead rise!

Each long, slow thigh infatuates
itself... each hand your back, each breast —
posed, self-besotted, you're obsessed
by mirrors where your languor waits.

One kiss from your mouth and I swoon,
to die. Your tongue thrusts weakness in
my heart, struck blind with awe and sin,
your mocking gaze calm as the moon....

Clinging to your instep's sultry
silk disdain, I throw beneath your feet
my joy, my genius, my fate —
abject with lust, the price is paltry....

You are all colour, meaning, light
to me! You make my damned soul beat
like a nerve — Explosion of blood heat
in my black, Siberian night!

(after Baudelaire)

Criseyde's Dream

And out hire herte he rente, and that anon,
And dide his herte into hire brest to gon,
Of which she nought agroos, ne nothyng smerte;
And forth he fleigh, with herte left for herte.
            (Chaucer: *Troilus & Criseyde*, Bk 2)

In the dream, a fish-eagle
feathered white as bone
stooped with its talons to her breast,
and searched there, and tore out
the thrusting heart —
that muscle clenching
and unclenching like a fist —
leaving its own
where hers had been,
one for another....

She'd felt nothing
of those claws wrenching
and slipping in her.... But had heard,
faint as the sea, the stiff-fletched, white, angelic wings
beating the air... and, dimly, seen
the great white bird
flapping and settling
on her, hunching
watchfully over the strong, furred
shanks and predatory
feet that worked within,
the fierce, resentful eye...
as if over the huge insatiate fledglings
screaming in the nest,
or carrion prey....

And then the great fish-eagle thrust
the air steeply to flight, and soared,
and bore the bloody heart away....

Within her chest,
her heart was aquiline, that of a bird.

Angoisse

Though you are innocent at least
of such things as remorse, you know,
like me, as much as any of the dead
of nothingness. But you don't have
bad dreams to haunt you. You have ceased
to dream. So, each of us will come, then go,
perhaps return... but never reach your head.

No matter to you I'm just here to save
myself from death, to wrest
some moment of my being leaking off in slow unrest.
Within the easy ignominy of this
body's will to shame, I lean to kiss
us to lubricity and drouth
on the slow poison of your quick, red mouth.

(after Mallarmé)

Sisera and Jael

The sun shone like a dark thing
through the roof's weft; the safety of the tent
smelled clean, of hemp,
like a new sack.

At the end of thirst
from stumbling over rock and slithering
down dry screes pouring like bits of broken bottles,
he'd begged for water
like some crownless, fleeing king.

And she, the woman,
was nervous, watchful, hospitable:
like a woman living without
a man, a tent pegged out alone
in the high blue desert air
under barren mountain-passes
of red Sinai stone.

He waited for the water: she squeezed milk
out of the tethered goat. She brought him butter
in a white-glazed dish.

He had begun to look at her....
But she'd already seen him dead.

When he slept, she took a flat stone in
her hand and hammered a tent-pin
like a piton through his head.

Gwlad, Gwlad

Far from the old landed
recusant genealogies behind
their diapered brickwork
and stagged-oak deerpark,

here even God's low-church,
the damp-ridden chapels
built on proletarian pence
and shopkeeper's shilling

where all stand equal
in their own sight and
preferred in His, refusal
bred like rickets in the bone:

a people so stiffnecked,
yea, verily into sullenness,
they'll duck to advantage
but look up to no man.

Gothic Cathedral

The round-shouldered stone
cuneiforms

that held the arc
bowed down by

weight unhooped and lifted
to acuteness;

growing tall, they earthed mass.
The load

passed into the ground
like electricity

along green copper.
Glasswork

broke the rainbow's
arch into

its parts and brought
them

in. God
already was dying.

And the monument,
built high about these

apertures
shaped like Dürer's pious, arthritic,

praying hands
(fingers uninterdigitating

upward, pressing
to an apex) drew down grace

to more
fervent fingertips.

The stone strained
like a tent filling with wind of wings,

of prayer become will.
The walls had shed themselves, were

weightless. Flying
buttresses anchored them

outside like guyropes.

Aquarium du Trocadéro

Here, in the terraced
gardens under the Musée de l'Homme
the stupefied,
reluctant fish stir behind glass.

The giant eel
swims 2 or 3 years
to reach the shallows
of its native river —

undulant, undinal
arrow of its unintelligible yearning,
it swallowed the Atlantic Ocean
through the slow
pulse at the gills.

Coiled like the Serpent
now in its illuminated, underwater tree
it is sleeping or dead.

The elvers
wave like weed. Born
in the tank, are they
incapable of memory or desire?

They mouth
the mollusc in the womb of rock,
like leeches.
The world blurs at the window.
They are at the source.

At other windows, tiny perch
hang
motionless,
like mobiles in the airless water,

and the sullen rainbow trout swerve
listless circuits
of their circulated tank.

The ferocious, brindled
pike cruise.

They have the neurasthenic, mad grin
and the water-cooled nervous system
of the Hollywood killer.
Here they dull like the fish in a case.

The fronts of the lighted tanks
are like Cinemascope screens in the dim light.

Lugubrious sunfish steer
towards the glass.

Found in the Garonne or the Pacific
currents, taken
from the cold Humboldt or the warm Gulf Stream,
the amnesic, doped fish wait.

Survivors of the Flood,
their boredom is cold-blooded
and absolute.
They are in their element.

Snake Park, Kenya

The lovely Green Mamba and the Puff Adder
hibernate in their dirt

and the Giant Python
black, one hundred pounds, a tiny
polished-stone glans-head
lost in a nest of thigh-thick coils
dreams and digests its bait.

Every time you gasp breath out
it slides and torques,
swift, terminal asthma tightening
till you can't breathe in....

Even the sleeping snakes are deadly
but here only the Spitting Cobra
is not bored numb.

More accurate than a quid-chewer, faster
than a camera, it spits
venom to blind
before the fanged
death-strike.

It is all reflex.
Cantilevered head swaying triggered
behind its glass,
the unblinking bead
eyes watch everything, calculating
as an Arab trader's....

But most terrifying of all are the grey
crocodiles, the lizard-men
waiting in dust.

Immobile
primitive as things extinct —

vestigial legs and claws, the jaw
long as a pterodactyl's
with a sardonic, shrunken
look of toothless gums
whose teeth would drag a leg
off like a ragged saw.

Out of the egg they live over a hundred years,
reach twenty feet.

Now only the eyes are live: paler
than grapeflesh
than a cornered cat's, the slitted perpendicular
pupil narrower.

Lidded in wrinkled leather, their gaze
is lecherous and loveless, lit
with an inane grin.
Even here it is bright
with remotely recalled desire.
The motionless cruelty of the brain behind it
ticks, beyond conception.

Then the eye
films
complacently upon its secret.

That wizened, knowing
face grew old in swamps of prey, launching
itself down mud-slides
for the kill
before Cain or the Fall, before
the mud grew man.

Fatherhood

A man alone facing the useless sea,
waiting for evening, waiting for morning.
Children are out playing, but this man wants
a boy of his own to watch at play.
Each day over the water massive cloud
collapses like sand-castles, forms again, tinting
the children's faces. The sea will always be there.

Morning's a wound. Sun inches down
the sodden beach, clings tackily to nets and stones.
The man goes out into the sunlit gloom, and walks
along the sea. He doesn't look at the brown froth
that tries to climb the beach, and knows no rest.
At this hour, children are asleep
still, in the bed's warmth. At this hour, sleeping
in her bed's a woman, who'd make love
if she were not alone. Slowly the man strips
naked as that woman elsewhere, and walks down into
                                              the sea.

Then night, when the sea vanishes, and you
overhear the great vacuity under the stars. Children
in the reddish houses fall asleep,
and someone's crying. The man, exhausted with waiting,
lifts his eyes to those deaf stars.
At this hour there are women who undress a baby
and put him to bed. There's a woman in bed now,
pressed to a man. From the black window,
the raucous, asthmatic breathing of the shingle,
no one listening to it but the man,
who knows all the tedium of the sea.

(translated from Cesare Pavese)

Vanishing Point 3000

Colorblind.
Slow parallax

of fields unwheeling, of dead
standing trees. No sky.

The sky is a remote screen.
Landscape

falls away
like tall New York held in a fish-eye,

as the convex mirror
holds in the room's evasion

to its apex.
He lives at steady 70

and cools from 98.4.

A truck moves out
in Denver.

Insomniac,

outdistanced by the sun,
he will know cities at night

unmooring,
drifting port or starboard

from empty bypasses
desolate with lights.

Road and the machine
race disappearing

into opposite directions.

The mirror is empty.

Flashbacks. Earth spins east.

Nausea

Summer. Sunday. And carfull after car-
full of the family-dead parking to stare
behind spattered curvatures of dusty
glass in faint, hot reeks of petrol, children's
vomit, car upholstery, unfolding
tubular-frame nylon safari-chairs
on gravel verges stained like garage floors:
stopping for sandwiches, tinned fruit and tea
from thermoses in insulated cups....
The middle-aged, the elderly, the young,
more refugees than ever left Saigon —
from pallid TV screens struck dead by sun
through flowered curtains. The night's dark, film-noir
clarities already throb and draw in them like
an abscess, magnetic North.... A morose
solitary child, too old for his parents,
slumps in the back seat at a lay-by, watches
the cars blur past. They will go further. They
will go as far as you can. They will park
on the promenade, pointing towards the sea.

Snow at Dawn

Snow's fallen overnight. The insomniac stares
At the awaited dawn, while couples dream,
Are re-aroused, recouple. Infants scream
For milk the temperature of blood behind their bars
Or struggle due, late or untimely out of wombs.
The day rings, workmen rise. In the depôt
Dim lights come on in empty buses. Snow
Astonishes a million curtained rooms.
The tramp, the Stock Exchange sodality,
The poet and the TV personality
Wake to their newspapers. Snow tippexes the real
And edits out the world to the Ideal.
In hospital a pumped-out Suicide
Wakes to the taste of rubber and the smell
Of ether in a curtained bed, not Hell.
Last midnight's newspapers are read, unfurled
In early urban trains. Outside, dawn blues
To black-and-white at cuttings. Crossword clues.
A rape case. Bosnia. Snow. The Market news....
The darkness passes onward round the world,
Fleeing like cloud unshadowing a field.
Rubberised pneumatic doors hiss open, are re-sealed
At empty quays, as dead air rushes through
The tunnels. Halitosis, hair-oil, 'flu;
Last night's dead cigarette smoke; dull, scuffed shoes.
At each successive stop, a silent troop
Of mostly men debouch or enter. Arts. The pound
Is high. Some supermodel's breasts. The underground
Pursues its ordained, labyrinthine loop.

Near Tilbury Dock

I watch boys fishing the squalid Essex shore
opposite Gravesend —
fat, tidal Thames, colour of cement
slurry, always
downriver to filth.

Behind them the powerstation
on all four
stacks steams on
like a riverboat into the low east wind.
Sawdust seethes in a box at their feet.

They don't catch much in this water —
a day, half a day watching
a line that pales
away before it enters, pulling
it in again when they get bored.

They say there are flounder
but I've never seen one caught.
Occasionally they've landed the black
eels, twisting
like devils on the hook.
They throw them to
flail and dull
on the path's dirt and polished stones.

When you lift one up
the fins are fletched, like arrows.

The rods and spoon-shiny reels are
catalogue-new.

Mostly, though, they come here for the company, these
boys and men standing to cast
at intervals along
the rough-cast concrete flood-wall —

not talking but at least
without the guilt of loneliness.

Waiting on a blank, white day
like this for something
that draws nylon line out tight
and beats in the dust
is just a way of waiting.

Sometimes it's the same with words,
though this too has been said before.

Old Man in Scrumpy House

Straight back
into the bladder, where I grasp
and take its edge off,
where I process it to come out
pale, innocuous as lemonade, this
sweetish acid in my jar
that looks like murky piss.

This cuts like grass.
This is The Rough.

They throw dead
rats into the tuns for fermentation.
The corpses float sideways
for a day, dissolving — fur, teeth,
bones, disease, everything....

If I dropped
an old penny in this glass and left
it overnight, corrosive
salts would eat it clean.
By morning it would
gleam in the cloudy depths
like Rhinegold newly struck.

But it's cheap,

and my youth lies
in there somewhere, base metal
shining gilt to electrolysis
and my slow, hunching stare.
The sour apple is my slow fall
and fast stupefaction.

It's not much of a place,
this. But I fit in like the oak

moth with this dingy furniture, these
sticky tables, these walls
reverting
back through generations
to the drab hue of tobacco.

And at least it's bright here,
noisy, maudlin.

Home is where
the heart is and the sphincter rots.

Saloon Bar Drinker

Oblique & paler, colder through this cold red Bass
the slant of winter sunlight
dying through the urns & flowers,
pale as air, of frosted glass
where cigarettes coil blue smoke, rise & cloud:
the greyer I exhale dissolves, a pall —
its blueness in the coral of my lungs
like starfish in the Great Australian Bight,
the Barrier Reef.... A pressed electric bell
jars, the recess at three. Bar-murmur swells loud —
remote as sea-surge in a shell,
as voices shouting under water. Three hours
I've sat here, drowned alone. All
my clarities lactesce, inspissate, set
without you. The taste of spilt milk sours,
and surfaces like vomit. My dregs dull, flat.
My soles upon the stool lurch from the rungs.
In the mirror where I slide & swoon
the drunken eye is sad; & pale, diurnal light
of afternoon grows strange, unreal upon me,
like a rising fish: a lidless film lowers
or lifts back, a slow exposure where I gape to see.
Against the waistband now I slacken, fat.
I unsit, stand to sway
hunched in rigidity to empty rooms I rent.
Emerging, I swim lost into the afternoon.
I drink only to my decay,
while something hardens round me like cement.

Agony

I'll wander the streets till I'm dead tired,
I'll learn to live alone and look each passing face
straight in the eye and still be what I am.
This coolness ascending in me, searching through my veins,
is an awakening each morning that I've never felt
so real — except that I feel stronger
than my body, and a colder shiver comes each morning now.

The mornings I had at twenty are now far away.
And tomorrow, twenty-one: tomorrow I'll go out in
                                            the streets —
I remember every stone, and the layers of the sky.
From tomorrow people will start seeing me,
I'll walk straight, and perhaps I'll pause
to see myself in windows. There were mornings once
when I was young and didn't know it, didn't even know
that who was passing by was me — a woman, mistress
of herself. The scrawny girl I used to be
was awakened by a weeping that went on for years.
Now it's as if that grieving never was.

And all I want are colours. Colours don't weep,
they're like an awakening: tomorrow colours
will return. Every woman will go out into the street,
each body a colour — even the children.
And this body of mine, dressed after so much paleness
in a frivolous red, will repossess its life.
I'll feel glances slide over me
and I'll know I'm me: a sidelong look
and I'll see I'm there, among people. Each new morning
I'll go out into the streets and look for colours.

(translated from Cesare Pavese)

The Avatar of King David

Sightseers now stroll Dachau, Auschwitz,
    Where we slid in pits,
   Live Jews already skeleton;
    Where troupes herd in
  Under the showers still, as for the Sistine
Roof. Marvelling faces lift, to stare upon
These concrete ceilings fingers clawed,
    To die. The Lord
   Was no sustain. No blessing flowed
    On millions. Smoke
  We rose as, and the elders' teeth they broke
For fillings.... They came on this road

I leave by through the gate, and stayed;
    Their bodies weighed
   By air, so light they rose as one:
    Like souls. This home
  Of their soul's dream crowds like St Peter's dome:
Their ceiling's here, where cameras click. Undone
They died here, and the ovens choked
    With ash. As smoke
   They rose to Israel.... I walk back
    And drive off, passing
  Cars queued to arrive, like traffic massing
To an aircrash; and their fumes are black.

Widow

Christmas roses wreath the bed,
brittle chrysanthemums.
The garden benches of hardwood
oak grey and
weather, empty. Wet dead

leaves litter the wet lawn.
But I become
invisible as the pure pane,
where a wave
ripples across still water. I'm alone,

the garden distorts in the flaws.
In the blank
exteriors always there's
only sky
framed: blind upward mirrors

of moving cloud. I'm an address
for sympathies.
Only the woman comes in twice
a week, and goes.
Then something panting, breathless

listens here — as quietly as must
the audible,
asthmatic breath of God. I'm fast
here; while,
circling slower than dust

motes in trapped sun, the walled air
swallows me in
a yawn that screams higher
than silence,
dead as the air in a jar.

When I go to the glass
window, I vanish.

Mississippi

I

The river in old age meandered
through the country's youth,
our dreamfed adolescence.
The bright, green maps, the
starry contour charts of soundings,
ink-wash, almost useless: obsolete
before they reached the colourist's:
shrugged from with a subtle twist,
like snakeskin.

Archipelago and bank dissolve or form....

A hundred years of printed maps
are collocated to a stiff spine: lift
and let the edges flutter down
beneath the thumb, and watch
it slowly animate, writhe
and digest, the line of river: supple, blue,
a thing alive.

II

The river in three days
threw up and beached
new townships on new bends,
as corpses rise, slow fish, for quicksilver
and bread strewn on the waters....
a single street churned up with mud,
a few days' hammering, cardboard facades....
The river god ignored their claim,
deserted them, and they died

back to landlocked hamlets, warm alluvium
drying out to dust and farming, stranding

ports in silt and leaving
harbours empty dry-docks, rotting jetties
overhanging flats of tidal mud, and sand....
The turtles' eggs left buried there hatched out
a mile inland.

III

Orange at neap, the vast sea-mile of river,
wide under that flat, white sky
and swollen, races cambered
like a roadway in its curbs, fattens with mud
the shoals of current swirled away
from what they snatch at, torn
meniscuses of sullen swells
cowed by uneasy winds....

Eroded banks collapse, abruptly liquefy to sand....

The marauding river-god scatters,
overwhelms the land, flooding
the dead acres, drowning dead grass,
bearing off the levy on its poverty:
live sheep and chickens, chicken-coops,
and spars of timber torn from twisted nails....

You skiff where there was labour, navigate
by houses, solitary trees, strange islands....

Like lights
shouts shiver on the water
through these nights....

IV

Glutted, the river-god sinks back
through the bedraggled vegetation, leaving
to your clung boots and choked heart
the catalogue of loss, the
devastated home. Fields clog with slurry
drowning detritus again. Those scraggy carcasses
black mud will bury.

V

But within a week that waste
of fetid mud would crumble to your fingers
soft, black loam,
as moist as fruit-cake,
would be dull with greenness
sweetly fledging it.... The
sign-stakes, fence-posts even
— dragged loose, levered crazy
in the changing swirls of flood, about
to spurn up earth — begin to put forth
their vestigial buds of branch,
to send out
strong, retentive roots that forked down
through the soil like lightning
from their seasoned sloth:

in sudden, atavistic Spring, that humid air
electric with their growth.

The Sunflower

Bring me the sunflower, so I can transplant it
to my own soil scorched with salt,
and all day long show to the mirrored blues
of sky the golden face of its anxiety.

Dark things turn towards clarity,
exhaust their corporal selves into a flux
of colours: thus, in music. And so, vanishing
becomes the one chance among chances.

Bring me the plant which leads you back
to where blonde transparencies arise
and life is vapourised as spirit;
bring me the sunflower maddened with the light.

(translated from Montale)

A Sense of the Passing
Thomas Hardy 1840-1928

Poor Hardy, haunting his own future, seeing
posterity in blown butterflies, the skeleton
in leaves, dead feet in the worn step....

Autumn weighed him not with ripeness
but decrepitude.
                        Winter
froze him like the stones froze
in the mud.
                        In Spring, all
that renewed was the past
and the past-to-be: ghosts already
mortal as his memory, the people
they had been.

                        And in Summer even
the steepling, foliaged elms
across a pasture were gone in the inappreciable
                        instant it took
light to reach his eyes, as if already
he saw
life as an old photograph of then:

the awkward, staring rural labourer,
lush-shadowed verdancy over his head;

the rings in this sawn stump.

Revolt

The dead man's convulsed, and isn't looking at the stars:
his hair's stuck to the pavement. The night's colder.
Those living get back home, still shuddering.
It's difficult to follow them, the way they scatter:
one bounds up stairs, another plunges down into a cellar;
a third goes on till dawn and then collapses
in a sunlit field. Tomorrow someone will smile
bitterly, in work. Then even that will pass.

Asleep, they look dead too: when there's a woman there
their smell is ranker, but they still look dead.
Each body's tight, convulsed upon its bed
as on the red pavement: the long exhaustion
until dawn is like the briefer throes of dying.
Over each body a sordid darkness thickens —
but not on that man dead, prostrate under those stars.

Even the heap of rags, warmed by the sun
and propped against a wall, looks dead. Sleeping
on the street shows trust in the world.
Among the rags, a beard, flies
swarming over it; while passers-by swarm in the street
like flies: the beggar's just part of the street.
Poverty, like grass, has overgrown his grimace
with a beard, gives him a peaceful look. This old man,
who any night could die, convulsed, in blood,
seems on the contrary a living thing. So, everything
is just part of the street, except the blood....
But the stars have seen that blood there on the street.

(translated from Cesare Pavese)

A Generation

A boy used to come to play in the fields
the outskirts have stretched over now. He found other kids
there, shoeless like himself, and he'd scamper free, in joy.
Running barefoot in the grass with them was fun.
One dusk of distant lights they heard gunfire crackle
in the city, and a clamour of panic reached them,
intermittent on the wind. They all fell quiet.
The hillsides swarmed with points of light, fanned
to a glow by the wind. Then darkening
night at last extinguished everything,
until only the freshness of the wind outlasted sleep.

(Tomorrow morning they drift back to truancy, the boys:
no one remembers what they heard. There are workmen
                                            in prison,
silent, and already someone's dead.
They've covered up the bloodstains in the streets.
The city comes awake, as if from far away, to sunlight.
People leave the house. They look each other in the face.)
The boys thought of the darkness in the fields,
and looked in women's faces. And the women
were saying nothing, and just let them look.
The boys thought of the darkness in the fields,
where girls came too. Making girls cry
in the dark was fun. We were those boys.
We liked the city by day: at night, just being quiet,
watching the distant lights, and listening to the murmur.

Boys are still playing in the fields there
where the streets have reached. And the night's the same.
You can smell the scent of grass as you go past.
The men in prison are the same men. And there are women,
just like then, who make babies and say nothing.

              (translated from Cesare Pavese)

Tristia: a Poem for St David's Day

*It profit a man not to give his soul for the whole world.
But for* Wales?   (*A Man For All Seasons*)

Robertson Davies (big-bearded
actor, playwright, novelist;
b. Thamesville, Ontario, 1913)
on a visit to Wales recounted

ironically how (in spoof
secondary nationalism,
or atavistic pride of surname)
on a whim one March 1st

he hung out a Red Dragon
and some Canadian university
colleague said: *That flag —
what country's is it? Burma?*

At one — the odd
sporting fixture aside —
with Dr Johnson as to what is
"the last refuge of the scoundrel",

retelling the Grand Old Ham's
droll anecdote's about
as close as I
like to come to patriotism too,

and for the annoyance (I only hope)
of our ironyless
and largely unsporting
homegrown patrioteers —

all those paravail churls and
jobards, jobsworths or
would-be placemen
who make it seem shameful

even to admit to
last night's private *tristia*:
getting maudlin and half-
drunk on *entre-deux-mers* and,

live on *France Musique*,
the quintessence of exile:
the Dvorák
of the New York years.

(Which they straight turned
to *Weltschmaltz*
film-scores,
aching for the prairies.)

Movietone

I

Warsaw, the camps too, that
eternal granular
grey drizzle
of old, jumpy newsreel:

and in Roman Vishniac's photos of the ghetto
the old woman in the headscarf
the inquisitive-eyed children
the family man

are arrested for us
as if held by gunsights: as if
already prefigured there, in 1938,
in those dark, Jewish stares, are those

who tottered out of sheds
in suits striped like pyjamas
all eyes and shaven head
in 1945, emerging

to the silence of the cine-camera's whir
dazed
as into too harsh light, emerging
like those who do not know why.

II

The frame is time
always, not space: the light
that of a day
imaginable, and almost remembered.

Ypres, the Rhondda marches, Munich,
the triumvirate dividing up the world at Yalta....
The past's a frame-up,
familiar

as those bandit-ridden wooded hills
round back-lot Hollywood,
or a job lot of Edwardian snaps, brown-studies
out of some old shoebox of the heart.

But light's vicarious
and instantaneous cheap
nostalgia leaves
no moral to record.

How find grief adequate to those
whom history spared neither
"what they could learn to endure"
nor what they could not?

Poem for Joseph, 10 days old

You were born
blue
as a skinned rabbit, slithering
out on blood and wincing

into air. Hard to recall the labour
of origins, conception
out of that stunned tumult
in the hospital at 3 a.m.

I watched the black midwife hold you
in clingfilmed hands
to clip a plastic clothes-peg
to your cord and snip

it, press
your scrotum for the balls
and launch
you: nameless, sound....

Harder still now, guessing
the tendentious and accident-prone
future, that private sum
of unimaginable concurrences

among quiddities and qualia
which elude
the act of writing to accrue
a life by seconds, inbreaths....

I watch air inure you daily, like a cut —
the soles of those tiny, miraculous, mauve feet
on which you have not stood
still tender as a glans-skin.

And the future's blank, the future's always
blank —
though that
says something for it.

Poem for Joe, December

Six months after the birth each
night hourly we go up
still to overhear
your breathing: stooping
into the dim cot, intent as
for the heartbeat.

Little egg, soft nape, unstirring
eyelashes, the pale fuzz
you were born with
shadows your head's
dome, profiled
perfect as a lightbulb's,

while your life
swings on that one, fine
hair
of imperceptible breath....
Until a tiny, sprawled hand
twitches, or (disturbed

between what dreams?) you lug
your head facing
the other way: four-legged
in your primrose
terry Baby-Gro,
still clumsy as a tortoise.

Gently I creak out backwards
on the floorboards.
For new parents each
child sleeps the sleep
of innocence and of
the just — the only just.

From *Black Faces, Red Mouths*

Pneumoconiosis

This is The Dust:

black diamond dust.

I had thirty years in it, boy,
a laughing red mouth
coming up to spit smuts black
into a handkerchief.

But it's had forty years
in me now:
so fine
you could inhale it
through a gag.
I'll die with it now.
It's in me,
like my blued scars.

But I try not to think about it.

I take things pretty easy, these days;
one step at a time.
Especially the stairs.
I try not to think about it.

I saw my own brother: rising,
dying in panic, gasping
worse than a hooked
carp drowning in air.
Every breath was his last
till the last.

I try not to think about it. But

know me by my slow step,
the occasional little cough, involuntary
and delicate as a consumptive's,

and my lung full of budgerigars.

Summer 1984

Sumer of strike and drought,
of miners' pickets standing on blond verges,
of food parcels and

hosepipe bans.... And as (or so
the newspapers reported it) five rainless
months somewhere disclosed

an archaeology of long-evicted
dwellings on a valley-floor, the reservoir
which drowned them

having slowly shrunk towards
a pond between crazed banks, the silted
houses still erect,

even, apparently, a dusty
bridge of stone you might still walk
across revealed intact

in that dry air, a thing not seen
for years; just so (though this the papers
did not say)

the weeks and months of strike saw
slowly and concurrently emerge in shabby
river-valleys in South Wales

— in Yorkshire too, and Durham,
Kent and Ayrshire — villages no longer
aggregates of dwellings

privatised by television, but
communities again, the rented videos and tapes
back in the shop,

fridge-freezers going back
— so little to put in them, anyway — and
meetings, meetings in their place,

in workmen's clubs and miners' welfare
halls, just as it had been once, communities
beleaguered but the closer,

the intenser for it, with resources
now distributed to need, and organised to last,
the dancefloors stacked

with foodstuffs like a dockside, as if
an atavistic common memory, an inheritance
perhaps long thought romantic,

like old men's proud and bitter
tales of 1926, was now being learnt again,
in grandchildren and

great-grandchildren of their bloodline:
a defiance and a unity which even sixty years
of almost being discounted never broke.

Onllwyn, West Glamorgan, 1985

"Pit" and "tip": the words were always more
than palindromic: synonyms. But
in Onllwyn here

by the ruinous, urinous pithead baths,
staring north across Tawe valley oakwoods
into the Beacons

National Park — filmic Montana backdrop
of ridge, escarpment, sky: crags
just inside Powys

today clear and close as if hung beyond
the brow of the far field, wrinkled fissures
in those rockfaces

as sharp, you imagine, as sometimes men saw
them on coming up, dark-faced
out of the dark,

resting pale eyes on distance, across
a white dazzlement of day — then turning to
the Banwen road, its

rough-cast cement-green postwar council houses,
chocked caravan, shop, pub, Welfare
Hall strung out under those

huge, still barely half-weed-grown dunes —
peaks apexed steep as if just poured
from the bucket dragline that

ran up from the drift over the grit-filthed
single street till 1961, the year
they shut the mine —

here, in this long hamlet lost in the dog-days
at the top of coal-tracked minor roads,
on the border of

coalfield synclines and conservationist Park,
bleakly wonder, stranger, as you
await a green bus out,

at what can only have been the contempt
for those who had to stay of those
who took out what

there was and went, like carpetbaggers, leaving
the rest to wind, rain and
the agency of birds.

Not even flattening it, you think. Not
even bulldozing or leaving the
bought seed to grass over

the mountainous geology of waste.

Miner, Abercynon, 1985

After we all went back
I was looking at the boys coming up
in the cage one day, he said,
at their faces and
white eyes, and knew
my own face was as black as
theirs and felt my own eyes
white and tired
in my head, and I
realised, That's it, that's how
it is to them, we're
black, the tribal
blacks of Britain.
When we go to work we're niggers.
When we go on strike we're reds.
The trouble is, he said,
and laughed — black face,
yellowed teeth, red mouth —
is that they see us
in such bloody primal colours.
And the only thing that's blue
about us — and he pulled
his sleeve-cuff back
to show me — is our scars.

In the Aftermath

What seems reallest
now is those early-morning
shots on fast
film or the newscasts
on infra red, flashing
police lights trailing
after-images
across the frame:
the men
in hundreds held back and
jeering impotently
at 5 or 6 or a dozen
being shuttled in.

Now, after all the lies
and rhetoric,
the sackings and the closures and the transfers,
the bitterness and
heartbreak and bravado and the sheer
exhaustion,
the names
persist in their own afterlife:

Cortonwood
Polmaise
Aberpergwm
Ashington
Treforgan...

Like a memorial
list on a faded honour scroll
of places, place-names
become famous the once
and already long ago,

or of places that are only names,
plain fields where battles were
fought, the names
become beautiful through
use and distance:

Edge Hill
perhaps, or Wagram
Chickamauga
or Thermopylae...

Only the names, inlaid
like legends.

So that now, and in what years
there are to come, men and
women may say, in their villages,
misremembering nothing
of what took place:

"Yes, I took wounds
in the sun at Orgreave".
Or, "I too stood
at the Phurnacite plant in Abercwmboi
penned and shoving, watched
that one man being driven
by a woman through
the gates under
the TV lights,
dawn after black dawn
in the terrible winter
of 1984-5".

From *Salt*

The Hook

I

I named it sickle. But he
uses it, the old man, and he called it:
the hook.

No longer new; a flatter curve
of blade than the gold on red: crescent
of an ellipse;

and implement, not emblem:
dull, rust oiled with usage; nicked, the
harshened silver edge.

But a tool perfects, almost
like nature, more stringent than art: millennia
winnowed to this

shape since Egypt was
the world's grainhouse, longer:
a moon-edge

cutting finer than a straight:
grass, not flesh: only the point would embed,
opening an enemy

like a full sack, or the edge hack
a limb, the swung fist past its mark;
but savage enough

a symbol of agronomy
for rising serfs. The crossed hammer beat
this out blue once

in a man's fist; but mass
produced now for a dwindling few, this tool,
this weapon:

the steel flattened, arched, made
keen, even the white ash turned smooth and
ferruled, by machine.

But finely weighted, this one:
light, as if I hefted only a handle, even
to the left hand,

even as it learns the backsweep.
I stooped and swung; the wristy, ambidextral hook
slew grass,

forestroke and back. I think
no eye bought this, but wrist: by balanced weight,
like grain;

and that it is beautiful only
now, for the coarse use that refined it,
like the sea-stone.

II

Beautiful too is the word:
swathe. I laid low all afternoon tall, green,
slender seeded grasses

of more elegance than poplars.
Their stems fell sheaved after the stroke
like armfuls of bluebells,

the blade was wet with sap.
Doubled I stooped, climbing the field
all the hot afternoon

for these red stigmata,
skinned blisters on the mounts of
both white palms.

October Oaks

It's work at morning
in a low, white field
of mist and three
October oaks.

Overnight the trenches gather
water, slip, refill.
Hidden like a gravedigger, I
work; ankled in mud, unfree.

The earth is heavy with
water. The sodden, black soil
drains it: a dark downward
secret, subterranean seepage.

The oaks drain earth,
suck salts. They have
a massive, hidden grip. Strength
knots their veins,

but it is failing.
The weight of the field
is immense. They hold
these acres until winter.

Drainlayer

I made these mountains
I undig and heave and
bury; laid
these ducts dry to the mains

with the statutory fall.
Now earth to earth, where
must return,
sure as the apple, all

things early. The blade
cuts clean, and brightens;
glazes earth
the downthrust frees, the spade

flings. But I bury my own
work dark. Nothing stands
but me.
I lay veins, straight bone

in earth for earth my daughter.
My hollow son is
earth too,
exoskeleton of water.

Ramsey Island

Drab gorse crouches;
and the stunted thorn, its back bent
from the lash, fleeing
the wind —
but root-bound,
like the girl becoming laurel.

There are no nymphs or gods pursuant
here;
hardly a crippled tree is bared
against the sky.

Only wind, running
the turf one way like a close pelt;
and precipices to the sea.

Even men, who root anywhere,
landed, lasted a few brute seasons out,
were gone.
There is nothing to grip on.

*

The island's a bird sanctuary now.
Like the leaning wind, it has
prevailed,
becoming finally what it always was.

The once-gutted stone
habitation has been renovated for the warden.
With his deep-freeze, radio and books,
his sinecure's
as steady as a lighthouse job.

He'll last here longer than those
who had to, and couldn't —

each crude, repetitive meal
earned
singly, eaten
after darkness off the day's bare plate —

the fish-taste of gull-eggs;
a rim of chipped bone.

*

Cut off in winter
for weeks at a stretch, you hunched to stare across
the straits and see
a man ploughing a field dark
on the mainland in a cloud of gulls,
as if on the next hill.

Here the dirt was
thinner than the scalp on your skull.

But there were worse straits —
the rock was
fast;
you thought of those out in that running sea.

A fine day
was not a respite but increase of labour.

Yet there were the moments: going
out at morning;
the sea sometimes, when the back straightened.

In a bleak, intermittent
diary, kept a full year he survived
on the island, Ivor Arnold, poor
at spelling and grudging

his entries
like flour or paraffin or twine,
recorded of a day in March, 1908:

"Wind S. A fine day. I could hear
Will Morris Pencarnan talking
to his horses yesterday from Congrwn Bach."

Pig-Farmer

Like boys who throw stones off the roadside
down on his stone-weighed tin roofs and pedal,
                    something in me flinches
at an uncouthness in this pig-farmer
guarding his triangle of black-tramped
mud between 2 ragged hedges and a stapled wire fence.

18 months ago or so he pulled into this
freehold, waste-ground
landscape like a lay-by. Now he lives in
a scrapyard compound
2 alsatians prowl on slip chains.
They're half-trained, and look half-starved — like the
        silence they dog, perhaps,
                sullen
                    ingratiating
                        vicious —
in 3 moves.

Beleaguered, padlocked by misanthropy, he's here
to stay —
even the yellow-and-white, second-hand caravan trailer's
now on 4 breeze-block piles
like a Portakabin classroom....

                    In it he must learn
infancy's difficulties every night over again, blunted
digits listed, totted, in the red
Silvine exercise-book with the moiré cover
and multiplication-tables on the back and metric
        measures:
11 eggs;
a refill blue steel Calor-gas bottle;
the dusty, hard hundredweight Portland cement-bags
        shouldered in still owed for....

Is this the sum
of all his sojourn, his
existence? —
         barely numerate
accountancy, bleak
monomania
among feed and dung, feed and dung
where only your own
labour comes free and unreckoned, you
buy always more than you can
find or sell, and you can't
get eggs from straw....

He put 2 youths, trespassers, in the hospital last week.

Even the silence is harsh
and suffocated in him.

Outside, the bedraggled donkey, the look
of life-long suffering on its greying
face, stands and outwaits
in its own breath
the patience of February drizzle
and a winter when every stick of timber —
the yard's sodden, inedible driftwood, the fence-posts,
        the slimy cobbled hen-house —
has turned green.

The midden of trodden mud
will never green under the trotters of his pink and filthy
    pigs....

24 hours they stink windward from their corrugated
    Nissen domes,
once daily jostling to waste

and tepid bran-mash —
>   vomit
rolled in sawdust.
Their new metal trough
is star-blue, frost-patterned from the galvanising.

But pigs, they say, find and eat
>   anything —
weeds; truffles of broken pottery grubbed
from the dirt; the dirt....
They'll crunch a corpse down past the signet-ring, the
>   severed
finger that denied them it —
>   then snuff their shit
for more....

There is a moment for his whole, partial
subsistence here to be imagined brutal, bare
and barbarous as that.

Then he straightens
his back —
his scarecrow coat knotted about the waist with
>   coarse, white hairy string —
and watches you stop looking at him and
go past.

Hill Farmer, Staring into his Fire

Aye, Ossie Jones can talk of wood, he thought,
weigh ash or beech or sycamore or this
or that, who gets it off a

pickup, block-sawn by the ton. And always he'll
say, smiling as if in a trance remembering
some snowy childhood

Christmas-time, Ah, but the finest log of all
to burn is apple — from, I suppose he
means, if he means anything

but common hearsay anyway, that orchard of grey
rough-barked russets, coxes, bramleys,
all older than himself,

that he had cut down for the space to sell to
build a bungalow, easy as bloody pie, forgetting
in the sweetness of that

smoke the flavour of the apple he can always
buy instead. Me, though, who'd no more
cut a sound

tree down than saw the arm off a young girl, I
think always of the dead wood not
the heartwood: trunks of

rotting birches mosses like stones: the one dry
limb on some old oak, crusted
with lichen stars: that

last peeled elmtree, white as bone, the wind
brought down one night: stunt
hawthorn from my hedging:

and the alder, the niggardly, prolific alder
that shoots up anywhere, or even likes
the poor-draining places,

and doesn't want to burn, you'd think it stayed
young wood out in the shed, or green or
damp for ever, it shrinks

so slow, burns so reluctant, as if it only bears
the flame from logs beneath it, red
with dying: like that one

uprooted one, and with just a one-man bow-saw —
twig and branch and trunk, aye, stump and
root as well, to keep the land

cleaned up a bit, and with buzzards coming
right down out of the hills
that year, like ponies —

that I lived a whole, long, bitter winter off.

New Land

The flints grate, turning up
to the spade's hacking, prising

edge — chalky, rounded
as the ball of

humerus or femur. This clay
hasn't been dug since

the sabre-tooths hunted Kent:
like shovelling rags

and old iron, a back-aching
frustrate work you have

to stand and survey
a minute every five.

The ochreous, white
flints chip

to glassy black
inside, obsidian.... I bend,

examine them, and fling
them in the barrow.

It's not the garden but the dream
of axe-heads

that keeps me digging.

Quarries at Dinorwic

I. The Hill

This is the black mountain
labour unpacked
so much, so long, it might have
built it:

ziggurat of terraces

precipitious pilgrimage of z-bend paths

poised avalanche of scree

fissle mud-stone home of the ancient, still-perfect

segmented trilobite

wall and roof

the industrial history of a region

metamorphic headstone of a village.

Mile-high litter
of slate.

II. The Workshops

The converted museum at its foot is still
positivistic for an occasional public
of holiday-makers and sixth-form groups:
as if the past were what is finished with.

Its old slate blocks are the green
of the mountain's lake.

Inside, a fetishisation of the primitive
pauses you
in workshops of used paraphernalia:
patterns, hammers, saxes, saws;
the broad, unique chisels;
the geometrical rectangled edge
of slates cropped by two single, expert blows.

Even the machinery has been made gentle
by the wear and shine of palms.

Nostalgia, too, in the old photograph, mist-bleak
of ruffian labourers
on the rubbish of shalings outside
their rubble hut.
A xeroxed newspaper text still speaks
of them, defunct,
of their defunct, particular skills
with parochial pride.

Now all this remains
to the tourist,
who is inheriting the earth:
a museum of dead
shops whose air was once dense,
smoke-acrid with breathable motes
and, outside, the leaning
slag-heap
of all they didn't finally carry away
in those rusty iron trolleys
or the intricateness
of the astonishing, pink lung.

III. The Graveyard in Dinorwic

Here things change slower than the yew-trees,

and the village's graveyard, steep at Boot Hill, still
shows in ranks
the rank of its dead:

a massive, glassy granite urn;
one blind, white angel
like the Victory on a Rolls; the plinths
and obelisks of vaults
guarded by railing spears....

Mostly, though, the cluttered, ordinary
headstones, all facing one way —
oblongs or Gothic-arch-shapes: slabbed slate
from the black hill.

Sometimes, to live in Wales is to know
that the dead still outnumber the living.

The chisel put your names in the blue slabs.
Wandering among them, I
taste only your anonymities
vicarious, bitter as brass —
accumulated
generations penned in
this village boneyard, herded
stones....

The chisel serifed your ages in the slate, too —
men dead in their 40s, the widows who outwaited them
for twenty years
by looking at the wall.

It was slate put you here.

The slate that can now never be wiped clean.

Navvies

The Poor Law Authorities had difficulties arising from the great Irish influx that took place between 1815 and 1846. There was a considerable influx from Scotland too, but the Northern emigration had little effect on the Poor Rates as the Scots were by nature frugal, provident and independent. It was otherwise with the Irish, and from 1820 to 1847 they were a heavy charge on the Poor Rate.... The vagrants were an expense to the Poor Rate in another way. Fevers and diseases were chronic in Ireland owing to the insanitary conditions in which the peasants lived. These diseases were brought over from Ireland, not only by vagrants, but by those who settled permanently in the towns as well.... Lancashire, the Liverpool and Manchester areas especially, were flooded with hordes of half-starved, half-naked Irish, spreading diseases wherever they went.

> (Briggs & Jordan: *Economic History of England*, 6th Edn., revised 1954.)

I

For the last time the aura emanates from the early photographs, in the fleeting expression of a human face. This is what constitutes their melancholy, incomparable beauty.

> (Walter Benjamin: *The Work of Art in the Age of Mechanical Reproduction*.)

**They still stare
out at us
    fixed, evasive
from the plate
in the museum case, the landscape they
inhabit fogged
       at the edges, vignette
without depth or recession, only an
                      oval**

of clodded earth their feet
stand on, like the grassy base
of a lead toy soldier:

a day's effort
            suspended, called away
to this
exterior —
enclosed and rustic-looking as a studio
pose, its slow exposure
                      held
long as an inbreath
can swell a burger's chest to pompousness, pull in
his lady wife's waist.

                Yet these women
plain, crude-featured, without
elegance, the dignification & parasol
of the studio posture, but thickened
by the labour
of work & birth,
                work &
birth,
in clumsy skirts, faces
expressing the strength of sunlight
above them
in a scowl, the lines of a frown
            almost as if it were anguish,
the mouths slack
& stupefied as if
astonished beyond all sense
either of insult or flattery
by the machine itself —
            something uncouth
about them all, as if they were jungle-
or prairie-Indians, these

nomads living & breeding in their litter
of shacks, illness & trampled mud
at the edge
of the road- or rail- or water-way they are
building and following, like gypsies....

The men at least more self-
aware, in a coarse-skinned
way: composed
and watchful from within what might be
resentment —
sharp-featured, hatted, with moustaches,
beards & waistcoats, so that
they might almost be rustlers,
like the James gang looked
in 1885 —
    but for clayed spades,
picks, and the navvie's yorks thonging
not holsters at the thigh
but mud-stiff trouser calves beneath the knee:
like working men
       caricatured
in old cartoons in *Punch*.

The plate is the ancient colour
of soot
   seen in sunlight.

Taken one
afternoon of now
unknowable
light in the second
half of the last
century, it is
the camera which unites
them for this

awkward
          class-photograph
they make....

Light and shadow; blur and grain —
                              yet eyes
beneath the hat brims, eyes
of labouring-men and
women, long dead but alive
in this, in
this
old scratched, ochreous monochrome
of nameless, graceless
strangers, standing so
uncomfortably, grouped without union
or conviction
          (while under skirts
of black, stiff cloth
the unseen
photographer — documentarist & no doubt something
of the sociological voyeur —
has withdrawn
into his concentrated, hooded
crouch, from where he gropes
to orchestrate them like a choir, define
them for his moment
and his age:
          a work-team
lined up, uneasy, in his frame,
excused labour for how long
it takes & then
disbanded back to it...

until they swim up in this
underdeveloped
print, out of a clearing
mist, a bleak, brown
drizzle,

                    as they were,
bodying
in chemicals as he saw them):

                miscellaneous rabble
crew, without connection
with each other
but for the composition
of this plate, a wage-list &
the speculation as to
                    which
of those men might be fornicating with
which women
in the shanties
they inhabit,

                without background
except for that
                    void
of pale gloom,
like a backcloth of
deprivation, ignorant
as all starved Ireland,
against which they stand,

                                with nothing,
in fact, but the tools
(if they carry them)
in their hands (if not, the hands)
and, as if keeping them
upright
            the workplace
of dim, photographed clods — the small
hummock, platform
of their existence
underneath their feet.

II. Tilbury Man

The forehead is long and narrow; the mid-line of the frontal bone extends from the beginning of the sagittal suture in a regular uninterrupted curve to the upper interval of the frontal sinuses, from above which interval, after a short slight concavity, the line is continued between the sinuses, again strongly convex, to the root of the nasals, which have coalesced with eath other and become anchylosed to the frontal bone.... There are no partial prominences of the frontal answering to those specified anthropomorphically as "eminences" in modern European skulls....

In the cranial part of the skeleton the indications of strong muscular characteristics (Plate III, fig. 3) contrast with the low cerebral ones (Ib., fig. 1) and like indications of brute force are given by the rest of the skeleton.

(Sir Richard Owen: *Antiquity of Man as Deduced from the Discovery of a Human Skeleton during the Excavations of the East and West India Dock Extensions at Tilbury, North Bank of the Thames.*)

        Found
        by some labourer, a man
                          unrecorded
        and now even more obscure
        than you are, who had to wait so long
        for this celebrity:

                        pocket of old bones
        34 feet down
        under the palimpsest of history,
        a layer-cake:

                grey tidal clay
                mud
                mud & peat
                peat
                mud
                peat
                mud
                mud & peat

                    sand & decayed wood
                    sand —

        cache
that had seemed fixed
rigid, impacted
in matter endlessly

                    (as slowly tumbling blimps
                    of severed astronauts
                    may one day wander
                    space,
                            unageing, dead, bodies
                    eternally at loose
                    shrivelling
                    in their fitted, miraculous suits,
                    faces shrunk
                    behind domed plexiglass):

tibias; a humerus; pieces
& chippings of this & that; a jawbone
(3 worn teeth were found that fitted it);
some ribs; an unusual femur:

found
at what had been
                a surface level
as if, you imagine, on a table of
clean, swept sand
with, perhaps, that primitive shattered
skull sitting in the middle of
its bones

                    (like the head
                    of a squatted African child,
                                        balanced
                    but too heavy almost to be borne

       among
       her rags & folded sticks):

as if the earth itself were
a ladder
some must climb back down, to
uncover
in a normal day's
slavery among oozing shuttering
and primal mud
something
that must have seemed like a desecration,
an unintermitted curse that had been
preparing itself against
that very moment for millennia:

                    a grave
not only unmarked
and anonymous, but laid down
even before the ownership
of names.

III

The dock labourers are a striking instance of mere brute force with brute appetites. This class of labourer is as unskilled as the power of a hurricane. Mere muscle power is all that is needed: hence, every human locomotive is capable of working there.

      (Henry Mayhew: "The Dock Labourers", in
      Mayhew's London.)

History is full
            of silences,
and they
seem as dead and abstract
to the world as

Paleolithic Man, these
Victorian labourers, vagrant
Irish slithering on treadmills
of trampled mud to bale
a wooden bucket full
of slurry while the water
rose to fill
each suck-hole
after them.

       Their graves
can be located
here and there:
               In Grays or Gravesend
or on the hill in Chadwell,
under the crazy stones and dead
grass of the subsided
churchyard whose consecration has now
run out, like a lease.
Some of their names
can be discovered
in the local paper of the day
(after 1886, on microfilm
in the Grays Public Library) —
mostly their deaths or accidents
at work, their drunkennesses,
petty crimes....

       But otherwise
it is as if they disappeared
for ever, with no surviving
public trace of
their existence, the nature
of their work, their passing.
               Only the work
itself remains:
          the cuttings, docks, canals....

As, when unknown prisoners
died in the permafrosts
of GULAG,
          the walls, buildings & watch-towers
they had been driven out
to build in order
to contain themselves
                  outlasted
them, their anonymity.

IV

The struggle of man against power is the struggle of memory against forgetting.

      (Milan Kundera: *The Book of Laughter and Forgetting*.)

Primitives, a slave-class,
they left no
bone arrowheads and coins;
no bronze-frail
helmet, edges
brittle as a dry leaf's
in the dints;
not even pot-shards.
                  Orphans
of both tradition and technology,
pure artisans, they
knew no smith's art past a tinker's cuss,
no skill in wood
or earthenware.

They shifted
         earth

deadweight, in cubic yards.

Illiterates, they had no voice
but quotidian speech
& the old songs, blind
songs, songs of
courtship, love, seduction, songs
of home:

a world
        warped
to the sentimentality
of atavisms, sung
in stillness,
hunched, rapt, with the eyes
closed:

        old songs
sung
into silence and against it,
                              unaccompanied
lamentation dying on the air
in exile,

        while its throbbing pathos ached
in the throat almost like tears.

Cold-Chisel

Cold-
chisel; bar; hexagon
of steel,
        you
put pressure
to the world through
a hammer-blow earthed
through a fist —

        searching
for the weak
point
in old, reverberant
brickwork, for
        fulcrum: to shatter
or prise,

        or flake
superfluity of marble to
        shape
out of a litter
of white chippings, and,
        angled, chase
the finest crease of skin under an eyelid.

Dropped, you clink.
You are the thing
that nothing hammers flat.

Blunt
or delicate,
by need,
        you
form and dismantle,
like good writing
should:
        cold-chisel.

From Lament of the Mechanical Excavator

Poor as a Colosseum cat,
I lived in the suburbs all lime
and cement dust, far from the city

and the country, crushed each day
in a ramshackle bus,
and every going and return

a calvary of sweat and of anxiety.
Long walks in warm fog,
long dusks in front of papers

heaped up on the table, through streets of mud,
low walls, shacks wet with lime
and without fittings, curtains up for doors....

The olive-seller and the rag-and-bone man
from some other district,
touting dust-dulled merchandise

like stolen goods, went past; and the cruel faces
of boys aged among the vices
of whoever has a hard, famished mother.

Renewed by a world itself new,
free — a flame, a breath I cannot describe
gave a sense of serene pity

to that humble, filthy, confused
and immense reality
teeming on the southern fringe.

A soul inside of me, that was not only mine,
a little soul in that unconfined world,
grew up, nourished on the joy

of one who loved, even if not loved back.
And everything was illuminated, by this love
perhaps heroically still adolescent,

and yet matured with the experience
that is born at the feet of history.
I was at the centre of that world

of sad, bedouin shanties
and yellow grasslands worn bare
by a wind always without repose

that came off the hot sea at Fiumicino,
or from the plain, where the city is lost
among hovels: a world

where the only thing that could dominate —
square, yellowish spectre
in the yellowish haze,

perforated, row on row, by thousands of
identical barred windows — was the Penitentiary
amid the worked-out fields and torpid hamlets....

Litter and dust, that the blind wind
dragged hither and thither,
poverty-stricken voices, without echoes,

of slatterns come here from the Sabine
Mountains or the Adriatic,
henceforth to camp here with their herds

of wasted, tough and strident kids
in ragged singlets
and greyish, faded trousers,

African sun and boiling rains
that made the streets mud torrents,
the buses foundered on some corner

at the last stop on the line
between a final strip of white grass
and some acidic, smouldering tip....

This was the centre of the world, just as
at the centrepoint of history was my love
for it: and in that

maturity that, in being born,
was still love, everything was
about to become clear — already was

clear. That suburb naked to the wind,
and neither Roman, nor southern,
nor working-class, was life

in its most actual light:
life, and light of life, full
in the chaos that is not yet proletarian,

as the Cell's rough newspapers
would have it, in their latest
fluttering of cyclostyles: but bone

of everyday existence,
pure in its being all too
close, absolute in its being

human, all too miserably human.

(traslated from Pier Paolo Pasolini)

Oxford Poems

I. The Colleges

After all these years, this place believes
In its myth. Outside, bright air burns colder.
The late afternoon intensifies. Golder
The sun gilds yellow stone and mottled leaves

Of tinted, tainted elms dying in drifts
On college lawns. Indian Summer will soon pass
Into another term, another Michaelmas.
High, in Agfacolour blue, the last swifts

Wheel, while visitors stroll quadrangles, to stare
In at small austerities of privilege —
The draughty common sink, the crumbling edge
Of Cotswold sills, the old decrepit stair —

Glimpsed in the tourism of mere spending-power,
Vicariousness on pilgrimage. While Nikons click
At Magdalen's deer, or Keble's Fairisle-pattern brick,
Even our own eyes mist at the worn step, arch, tower,

Long blurred by envy, arrivisme, regret
In our own complex retrograde emotions
For a lifestyle of which life here lends us notions,
Nostalgia for false worlds we've never met,

Yet to which so many hunger to belong —
All still persisting through a silvered, Georgian haze
Across meadows, trees heavy with shade: such days
As only Oxford's midsummers prolong.

II. Outside the Hospital

Perimetered by rosebushes, the grass
Outside the Cowley Road General Hospital
Is strewn with news, red sunlight, butt-ends, spittle,
Glass. Two women in saris pass

By fallen, or clutched, or broken bottles
And their drinkers, huddled to intermittent talk
Or reverie. One climbs upright, totters to walk
Elsewhere, and stain a quiet wall. The glottal

Muscles work their udder, rhythmic throat full
Back, the dark flagon upending in the fist.
He lurches. Deliberates the label (he's kissed
Three goodbye, since two). His sleeve's scagged. Life is
       wool,

Unravelling. He stares about in the agonised light.
The empty joins the refuse — Cyprus sherry,
Strongbow quarts: wet-nurses to needs less merry
Than morose. It's colder. Two Irish fight

Slowly, for money back on bottles one found
In the flowers. They're joined, parted, by a third.
The young copper contemplates, defers, a word.
More empties now than full ones, smashed than sound,

Scatter the grass. Even drinking cannot fix
Drink's brief exultancy, the failed fervour of years.
Its full, sad joy swelled in the chest like tears.
The pubs open the doors again at six.

III. The New Estate

Vandalism's just destruction of the Thing, speaks
Out of inarticulacy's hatred, blind,
Without objective but mute objects it must find,
Yet not finding itself in what it breaks

Or scrawls miss-spelled obscenities across —
Discovering neither self nor thing — it tries
To break free from a spell, to personalise
Unfreedom through an act, to compensate a loss

Which is nothing less than that of the world,
Wounding the walls of council flats, the railed
Sapling, a parked Mercedes — a world entailed
Still — but just confirming namelessness through hurled

Initials, nicknames, blurted syllables
Like empty threats among the hoardings selling
Blandishments — anonymous, a voice yelling
For its autonomy, unkillable

But futile still, identity without a face,
Impotent as graffiti in the white-tiled
Toilet cells, speech of minds made brutal and defiled,
Despair held private in the public place

And no outlet for its rage and outrage
But through that crude art of defeat, where every man
Is made alone in his defiance, without plan
Or hopes, gnawing the bars of his steel cage.

Tartan Army

They come from these drab streets
beside a football-ground, or drabber,
or the terrible estates,

the ghettoes of Govan and Greenock,
coming the 400 miles in crammed coaches,
hire-cars, or a straggle of youths

thumbing it all night down the motorways,
many jacketless even (it had been
a fine day leaving, yesterday),

just shirts or logoed t-shirts for a
chill May Saturday, and rain, in Cardiff,
but remembering never

to forget their emblems and insignia,
the pom-pommed caps and tartan scarves,
the yellow lion-flags, coming

rough, sleepless and boisterous
and smelling stale with lunchtime beer,
these unmistakable

faces of a proletariat, their swelling
chants and banners striking an
atavistic nervousness into

the hearts of barricaded shopkeepers
and car-owners self-locked in
in helpless traffic queueing

stalled for them in Leckwith Rd, then
thronging past the policemen grouped
in threes beneath

the armoured railway bridge to watch
for any sign of trouble but knowing that
the urban underprivileged

are often noisy here but almost always
tame, the worst they'll do is get drunk
afterwards and brawl among

themselves, they haven't got more sense than
that, the bastards, and we've got
the dogs, that it's enough

for them to come and come together, just
to be there on the match-day to see
Charlie Nicholas and Gordon Strachan

run on. In those night-blue Scottish shirts.

August. Sunday. Gravesend.

I

Leeward
        of the cement-factory's fallout
the hawthorns are dust-
choked, whiter
        than blown willows, than
with may.
Quarry, yard, the corrugated
metal sheds are
white
like bakeries.
        Silence. A coupling
clinks. Lime
gags the suburb's throat. Heat
                settles
everywhere
through haze.

In time, a mix
of summer rains, the
hawthorn
petrifies.

II

The damp-drab concrete council houses whiten
like a bone
in sun. A back
lawn, worn
        to tufted dirt, rotating
litter.

Tyres. A toppled tricycle. A football of
black hexagons
        rolled, flaccid, to a halt.

It is like the moment after an explosion.

                                                Shards
of orange polypropylene —
a shattered toy
aeroplane —
            are laid down
in the lettuce-bed's dry clods.
They will outlast the Pyramids:

the archaeology

of childhood, its lifelong
amnesia.

III

The river
glitters beyond
a horizon
of cranes. In Essex a car
window flashes.
                    Each moment
glitters
like a dying mullet
for the boy —
            workless, too old
for school, kicking his toes thin
against a wall....

The day is timed by
                    brutal gum
turned in his mouth.
It is chewed grey, whorled
like a brain.

He will carry it
              all through a youth and stick
it every day beneath a table.

For him each day is
like a Sunday.

He has shaved
his head
blue as an armpit, and
wears badges.

Back to Cardiff

The homecoming was always the same, the landscape
growing meaner mile by mile, the yards
of the intervening
farms as sordid as a gipsy settlement,

moored in the roads
of trampled mud
and rusting motor spares, ditched cars.

There is no greenness, only
the yellow fallow of dead grass,
nomadic sheep lost in a huge, bare field,
the white gulls scavenging inland.

Decreptitude and rust follow
the railway like a shanty town, its rubbish
strewing a trail into the city.

Scott sailed from this city
when it was young,
to die in the white Antarctic,
underneath the world.

The California Gold Rush
was undertaken out of both hope and despair.

The river lifts and drops
at the mouth of the salt tide. Above banks
of the alluvial, olive mud

the ponies are bowed
all day to crop subsistence, broken
by boredom, lashed
by slant grey rain.

The landscape
crowds with hedges, council houses,
recreation grounds. I was young here,
in the truant, errant holiday of youth.

The train slides
through the backs of the city.

It was later I yearned, heartsick,
for green, academic Summers.
So things drift, to knot.

Where is the may, the white
may, and Midsummer's silver dream, lost
in the suburbs
and confronted with the Spring?

Living

Living touches us
strangely, as if with accidental
sadness:
          an old woman
buying a single onion
at a stall;
          the rust-frail
edge of corrugated-iron sheeting
and a mattress
disembowelled on a stretch
of waste ground;
          and
in the night a high, white moon
like a coin
from which the face is worn.

                        I record
these
facts beyond other comment,
only because it might be as if
they never were.

Evening

The path
wavers
like a bicycle across the field
its shaggy, worn furrow.

                        At the asphalt
pavement where the houses end
the man dismounts
for milk-bottles smashed
and ground to glitters
into the sun.

                A tyre hoops
eccentrically the single streetlamp's
foot.

      What does it touch, seeing
them, these
men in dark, old suits and cycle-clips,
with haircuts and haversacks,
still pedalling slowly from work?

Hot Estate Sunday

The man sits smoking on the step
in shorts, next to the righted racing-bike
stripped, oiled and cleaned.
A television set
surges amid gunfire
in the empty room, its blowy windows open.
To his own eye, looking down,
he's already browner
than he is, and the terracotta
chimney-pots now burn
with evening.
His kid plays on
the hairy scrap of lawn. It's half
in shadow.
When he finishes
this cigarette, he'll wheel the bike
inside and wash,
put on a clean coloured shirt
and take the slow
walk to the new, brick pub.
Sometimes he arrives
foot-perfect, as the bolts go back
at 7.
He'll drink tonight until the sky is black.

Cafe, Rainy Tuesday Morning

The boy keeps his cup of
dregs on the formica tabletop

in front of him as if
it were a ticket for admission.

He nurses it close to
his hands when the old man

comes clearing tables.
It's a white, semi-translucent

cup, the kind you always get
in cafes. People

go and come. But others
stay, like him. He's

not the only one. Today
he's got the table by the street.

He taps a wrinkled
cigarette made from the tin's dust.

The urn steams. The plateglass
steams. Again

he clears a segment
of it with his sleeve,

a windscreen-wiper's shape.
He's heading nowhere

fast, his father keeps on
telling him. He only knows it's slow,

too slow. It's not yet even
noon, and there's no future

in his tealeaves.
He bought *The Sun* this morning,

but it's rolled up
on the table near his cup. Now

and then absently he'll pick
it up and furl

it tighter in his two hands,
almost like you'd wring

a chicken's neck. The newsprint's
soiled

his fingers, but that's all
it's good for now. He

doesn't get it for the jobs. One
thing he's learning, that

it's hard to make a daily paper
last all day.

Pull-in

They know her, easy,
from the drab, ill-fitting shoes,
that sullen tough look or
one pale bare thigh's faint
blue nubeculae of bruise,

like thumbprints fading
out through hues of iodine.
She re-crosses those flagrant legs,
shifts gum across her mouth,
re-chews it. Sixteen? Seventeen?

The shoe-heel swings free
from her blackened, wrinkled sole,
a picked scab where the upper
must have worn her last
tights to a hole

just beneath the tendon.
Absently her toes flex
to the jukebox's dull base-line.
She waits on, hardly in time. What
she's rife with's not so much sex

as an aleatory boredom
up and down the motorways,
in gravel lorry-parks and Little Chefs.
The arm whirs, re-selects and
drops: Hendrix, and "Purple Haze".

Her youth's composed of
these anachronistic hits
made hers by proxy. She outstares
and then ignores you, as
her driver comes back, sits,

gets up to slot a coin
in the machine against the wall.
He sways, slams, joggles. She's sprung
flippers, bumpers, arches,
pivots. He's a shiny silver ball.

Notes

A few words on the several translations included in the early part of this volume:

Out of respect for his narrative strength and clarity, the liberties I've allowed myself in my versions of Pavese are few. But every translation which seeks to work, as poetry, in its second language is to some extent an "adaptation". And with some of my poems here my departures have been radical. For example in "Falsetto" I've restructured, reslanted, and omitted and invented freely — for a poem that is, finally, as much mine as Montale's. Even less remains of Mallarmé's "Angoisse", though his poem does lie at the origin of mine: I have perhaps only pointed, made less cerebral, what we would now call the sexism of the original. Baudelaire's "Chanson de l'Après-Midi" I have condensed somewhat — the only way I could get it to work for me in English.

Various other poems are derivations in a much more indirect sense; that is, they are "literary re-tellings". "Ulysses Becalmed", "Sisera and Jael" and "Criseyde's Dream" are instances of this: certain stories seem always susceptible of being told afresh in poetry.

For me, the accurate translation, the adaptation and the literary reworking are all grist to the same mill.

p. 41. "The Avatar of King David". Cf. Milton's version of the Third Psalm:

> I lay and slept, I wak'd again,
>   For my sustain
> Was the Lord. Of many millions
>   The populous rout
> I fear not though incamping round about
> They pitch against me thir pavilions.
>   Rise, Lord, save me my God; for thou
>   Hast smote ere now
>   On the cheek-bone all my foes,
>   Of men abhorr'd
>   Hast broke the teeth. This help was from the Lord;
> Thy blessing on thy people flows.

pp. 60-65 I've included in this volume several previously uncollected poems dealing with the 1984-5 Miners' Strike, which originally appeared in pamphlet publication (in *Black Faces, Red Mouths*). Some of these poems were written close to events during that bitter, long-drawn out yet climacteric strike — and written in the heat of compassion or outrage. Perhaps this is why I'm no longer sure if they entirely work as poems; but what they allude to was, for many people, part of the most intense, cataclysmic and divisive emergency to take place in domestic politics in Britain since the Second World War. And for this reason, if no other, I feel they should be included and left to stand as they are. Sometimes, in order to avoid self-revisionism, a poet should simply let his work bear witness to what he saw and thought at the time — leaving the testimony intact, as if made under oath.

p. 65 in "The Aftermath".
The running skirmishes between striking miners and mounted police took place at Orgreave Colliery, Yorkshire on a hot day in summer, 1984. Film of the occurrence, the most violent encounter of the year-long strike, was shown repeatedly on BBC TV news during that day and the days that followed. The grave-voiced BBC film report showed miners hurling stones and abuse, followed by shots of police on horseback charging, with batons drawn, as if in response to this provocation. The batons were then seen deployed in what might be called liberal use. I still recall standing up out of my chair in astonishment and horror at seeing a man I knew, Philip James of Coelbren, take a blow to the head from an officer on horseback and then, while stunned and holding the visibly bleeding wound, suffer arrest, on national television, by other officers.

It was later established that the true sequence of events had been reversed in a BBC editing-suite: in reality, the mounted police (in full riot-control uniform, with shields and batons) had charged into the ranks of miners (on foot, unarmed, and "in daps and t-shirts"), who had fallen back in broken order and, only at that point, begun throwing whatever missiles came to hand.

The solidarity of the strike at the mephitic, coaldust-black (and now largely dismantled) Phurnacite plant in the Cynon Valley, Mid-Glamorgan, was broken by a single employee, whose wife drove him to work each morning for the six o'clock shift. This insistently ordinary and everyday marital arrangement was met daily by hundreds of pickets who turned out at the factory gate in an effort to prevent the husband's arrival for work, and who were themselves held back by almost as many police. Night after night we sat and watched this struggle — no less bitter because everybody knew it was symbolic — in local news broadcasts on our television screens.

These explanations may be of largely historical interest now. But it was by such images as these that hearts were impassioned or brought close to breaking point.

Acknowledgements

Some of the poems in this collection originally appeared in the following magazines, publications and anthologies:

Ambit, Arcade, Archive (USA), *Anglo-Welsh Review, Anglo-Welsh Poetry 1480-1980* (Seren), *Cumberland Poetry Review* (USA), "Dial a Poem" Service of the South East Wales Arts Association, *Element 5, Ffotoview, The Future of the Word, Green Horse, Nostos, Outposts, Poems '74, Poetry Dimension 3, Poetry Southeast, Poetry Wales, Prospect, Radical Wales, Southeast Arts Review, Stand, Straight Lines, Three Young Anglo-Welsh Poets, Voices* from *Arts for Labour.*

"Pneumoconiosis" was read on BBC Radio 3 and Radio 4; "The Hook" on BBC 2TV's *Closedown*; "Summer, 1984" on HTV's *Workers of the Word*. Many of these poems were read on G.B. Radio, Newport, Gwent, when the author was Writer in residence at the station. The opening poem of "Navvies" was awarded the Barbara Campion Memorial Prize for Poetry, 1982.

Translations of Pavese by permission of Peter Owen.